KT-230-025

EXTREME ANIMALS

CRAZY CREEPY CRAWLIES

Isabel Thomas

WAKEFIELD LIBRARIES

30000010254952

www.raintreepublishers.co.uk
Visit our website to find out more information about Raintree books.

To order:
☎ Phone 0845 6044371
📄 Fax +44 (0) 1865 312263
💻 Email myorders@raintreepublishers.co.uk

Customers from outside the UK please telephone +44 1865 312262

Raintree is an imprint of Capstone Global Library Limited, a company incorporated in England and Wales having its registered office at 7 Pilgrim Street, London, EC4V 6LB – Registered company number: 6695582

Text © Capstone Global Library Limited 2013
First published in hardback in 2013
Paperback edition first published in 2013
The moral rights of the proprietor have been asserted.

All rights reserved. No part of this publication may be reproduced in any form or by any means (including photocopying or storing it in any medium by electronic means and whether or not transiently or incidentally to some other use of this publication) without the written permission of the copyright owner, except in accordance with the provisions of the Copyright, Designs and Patents Act 1988 or under the terms of a licence issued by the Copyright Licensing Agency, Saffron House, 6–10 Kirby Street, London EC1N 8TS (www.cla.co.uk). Applications for the copyright owner's written permission should be addressed to the publisher.

Edited by Daniel Nunn, John-Paul Wilkins, and Rebecca Rissman
Designed by Philippa Jenkins
Picture research by Elizabeth Alexander
Production by Victoria Fitzgerald
Originated by Capstone Global Library
Printed and bound in China by CTPS

ISBN 978 1 406 23777 1 (hardback)
16 15 14 13 12
10 9 8 7 6 5 4 3 2 1

ISBN 978 1 406 23783 2 (paperback)
17 16 15 14 13
10 9 8 7 6 5 4 3 2 1

British Library Cataloguing in Publication Data
Thomas, Isabel.
Crazy creepy crawlies. -- (Extreme animals)
595.7-dc22
A full catalogue record for this book is available from the British Library.

Acknowledgements
We would like to thank the following for permission to reproduce photographs: Alamy pp. 6(© mauritius images GmbH), 11(© Image Quest Marine), 13 (© Whitehead Images); Ardea.com p. 25 (© Auscape); Corbis p. 23 (© Frans Lanting); Dreamstime.com p. 26 (© Ryszard); FLPA pp. 18, 19 (Mark Moffett/Minden Pictures); Getty Images pp. 4 (Roger de la Harpe/Gallo Images), 12 (Frank Greenaway/Dorling Kindersley); Nature Picture Library p. 21 (© Doug Wechsler); NHPA pp. 14 (Daniel Heuclin), 15 (© Stephen Dalton), 27 (George Bernard); Photolibrary pp. 5, 16 (Satoshi Kuribayashi/OSF), 10 (Carlos Martínez/Age fotostock), 17 (John Mitchell/OSF), 22 (Gavriel Jecan/Age fotostock); Shutterstock pp. 7 (© Nick Stubbs), 8 (© Fong Kam Yee), 9 (© Horia Bogdan), 20 (© Smit), 24 (© EcoPrint).

Main cover photograph of a giant Asian mantis eating a cricket reproduced with permission of Shutterstock (© Cathy Keifer). Background cover photograph reproduced with permission of Shutterstock (© EW CHEE GUAN).

Every effort has been made to contact copyright holders of material reproduced in this book. Any omissions will be rectified in subsequent printings if notice is given to the publisher.

Disclaimer
All the Internet addresses (URLs) given in this book were valid at the time of going to press. However, due to the dynamic nature of the Internet, some addresses may have changed, or sites may have changed or ceased to exist since publication. While the author and publisher regret any inconvenience this may cause readers, no responsibility for any such changes can be accepted by either the author or the publisher.

Some words are shown in bold, **like this**. You can find out what they mean by looking in the glossary.

Contents

Extreme creepy crawlies 4

Beastly beetles. 6

Masters of disguise 10

Don't eat me!. 12

Super-strong silk. 14

Wicked wasps 18

Tiny but noisy. 20

Migrating monarchs 22

Terrifying teamwork 24

Record-breakers 28

Glossary. 30

Find out more 31

Index .32

Think you know everything about creepy crawlies? Think again! All creepy crawlies have hard outer bodies with squidgy insides. But the differences between them are what make them **extreme**.

thick-tailed scorpion

This Bombardier beetle has an extreme way to scare predators. It sprays boiling poison from its bottom!

Strange features or behaviour help creepy crawlies to find **mates** or food – or to avoid getting eaten themselves!

Beastly beetles

Visit almost any land **habitat**, and you'll find a beetle living there. There are more types of beetle than any other insect in the world. They come in many different shapes and sizes.

This Namib Desert beetle can catch water from fog on its wings. This helps the beetle to live in very dry places.

dung

DID YOU KNOW?
Dung beetles
feed on animal
droppings!

7

If there were a bug Olympics, beetles would be the stars. Australian tiger beetles are the world's fastest running insects. If they were human-sized, they would be able to beat a racing car going at top speed!

Mantises have amazing **camouflage**. The shapes and colours of their bodies match their **habitat**. This helps them to **ambush** their **prey**. Their big, spiny front legs are used to grab prey and stop it from getting away.

leaf-coloured wings

sharp spines

prey

DID YOU KNOW?
The orchid mantis
looks just like an
orchid flower!
Can you spot it?

Don't eat me!

Bugs may be snack-sized, but they don't want to be eaten. Centipedes and millipedes have some **extreme** ways to scare off **predators**. Millipedes squirt out poisonous chemicals when they are in danger.

centipede

This giant centipede's bright colours are a warning. "Don't try to eat me, I have poisonous fangs!"

DID YOU KNOW?

The shocking pink dragon millepede from Thailand is just three centimeters long. Its bright colour is a warning to predators to stay away.

13

Super-strong silk

Spider silk is stronger than steel, and tougher than a bulletproof vest! It is perfect for trapping fast-moving **prey**. In the Solomon Islands, people use the enormous webs of orb-web spiders as fishing nets.

bird caught in web

orb-web spider

DID YOU KNOW?

Baby spiders can fly using their silk. The wind can carry them thousands of kilometres!

Jumping spiders don't need webs. They can leap 50 times their own length. This is like a 100-metre sprinter leaping from the start to the finish line! The spiders' huge eyes help them land right on top of their **prey**.

The Goliath tarantula is the world's heaviest spider. It has even been known to eat birds!

Wicked wasps

The tarantula hawk wasp is a tarantula's worst nightmare! The wasp **paralyses** the tarantula with a sting so that it can't move. Then it drags it to its burrow, and lays an egg on it. When the egg hatches, the wasp **larva** eats the tarantula alive!

burrow

tarantula

wasp larva

19

Cicadas are the world's loudest insects. They **vibrate** little drum-like parts on their bodies to make a noise louder than thunder or trains!

noise-making drum

20

DID YOU KNOW?

Some cicadas spend their first 17 years underground. Hundreds of thousands of cicadas come to the surface at the same time to **mate**. They die after just two weeks.

Migrating monarchs

Imagine the chaos if everyone in Mexico decided to go on holiday to Canada at the same time! Every year, 100 million Monarch butterflies make this journey together. They **migrate** up to an incredible 4,500 kilometres!

Birds and other predators leave the butterflies alone. Baby butterflies eat milkweed, which makes them poisonous as adults.

Terrifying teamwork

Termites live in **colonies** of millions or billions. They are tiny, but they work together to build some of the biggest homes made by animals. Their mounds can be taller than a giraffe. They are made of earth, spit, and poo!

termite mound

DID YOU KNOW?
Australian termites munch through everything from wood and tyres, to electricity cables. They destroy houses and bridges.

Army ants are fearsome **predators**. They work in teams to attack much bigger animals. They swarm over anything in their path. They bite and sting their **prey** to death.

DID YOU KNOW?

The only way to escape army ants is to stay totally still. Army ants are blind. They can only find prey that is moving or making a noise.

Record-breakers

Which creepy crawly do you think is the most **extreme**? Why? Have a look at some of these record-breaking creepy crawlies to help you decide.

What? Giant huntsman spider

Why? World's largest spider

Wow! These megabeasts have a leg span of 30 centimetres – as long as a classroom ruler!

What? Australian tiger beetle

Why? Fastest-running insect

Wow! This super sprinter can travel 2.5 metres every second when chasing **prey**.

What? Goliath tarantula

Why? Longest fangs

Wow! These spiders have fangs up to 1 centimetre long. Their bite is painful, but not dangerous for humans.

What? Goliath beetle

Why? World's heaviest insect

Wow! They can weigh as much as a large apple.

What? Millipede

Why? Most legs

Wow! A Californian millipede holds the record for the most legs, with 375 pairs, or 750 legs!

What? Fairy fly

Why? World's smallest insect

Wow! The smallest males measure just $1/5$ of a millimetre. You could fit five on a full-stop on this page!

Glossary

ambush attack an animal from a hiding place

camouflage colours or markings that help an animal to blend in with the things around it

colony group of many animals of one kind that live together

dung animal droppings

extreme unusual, amazing, or different from normal

habitat natural home of an animal

larva insect in its first stage after hatching from an egg

mate come together to produce young. An animal's mate is the male or female it mates with.

migrate move from one place to another when the seasons change

paralyse take away the ability to move

predator animal that hunts other animals for food

prey animal that is hunted by another animal for food

vibrate cause something to make small back-and-forth movements that make a noise

Find out more

Books

Deadly Insects (Wild Predators), Andrew Solway (Raintree, 2005)

I Wonder Why Spiders Spin Webs and Other Questions about Creepy-Crawlies (I Wonder Why), Amanda O'Neill (Kingfisher, 2011)

Insects and Creepy-Crawlies (Explorers), Jinny Johnson (Kingfisher, 2011)

Websites

Watch army ants attack:
www.bbc.co.uk/nature/life/Eciton_burchellii#p0039z74

Watch videos of creepy crawlies and other animals:
kids.nationalgeographic.com/kids/animals/

Index

army ants 26–27
Australian tiger beetles 8, 28

beetles 5, 6–9, 28, 29
bird-eating spiders 29
bombardier beetles 5

centipedes 12
cicadas 20–21

dung beetles 7

fairy flies 29
food 5, 7, 18, 23

giant huntsman spiders 28
Goliath beetles 29
Goliath tarantulas 17

jumping spiders 16
larvae 19, 23

mantises 10–11
millipedes 12, 13, 29
Monarch butterflies 22–23

Namib Desert beetles 6

orb-web spiders 14
orchid mantises 11

poison 5, 12, 23
predators 5, 12, 13
prey 10, 14, 16, 26

rhinoceros beetles 9

spider silk 14, 15
spiders 14–17, 18, 19, 28, 29

tarantula hawk wasps 18–19
tarantulas 17, 18, 19
termites 24–25